To Anton and Matthew, with love

A special thanks to Don Loney, Sandra Tooze, Helge Hongisto, David Densmore, the librarians at the Oakville Public Library, the Sheridan College Library and the University of Windsor Library for their help in producing this book.

Table of Contents

DISCOVERING CANADA

The Vikings

ROBERT LIVESEY & A.G. SMITH

Stoddart

First published in 1989 by
Stoddart Publishing Co. Limited
34 Lesmill Road
Toronto, Canada
M3B 2T6

CANADIAN CATALOGUING IN PUBLICATION DATA

Livesey, Robert, 1940-
   The Vikings

Includes index.

(Discovering Canada series)
ISBN 0-7737-5209-9

1. Vikings - Juvenile literature.   2. America - Discovery and exploration - Norse - Juvenile literature.   I. Smith, A.G. (Albert Gray), 1945-   .
II. Title.   III. Series.

DL65.L52 1989   j948'.02   C88-095363-2

TEXT ILLUSTRATIONS: A.G. Smith
COVER ILLUSTRATION: Wes Lowe
COVER DESIGN: Brant Cowie/ArtPlus Limited
TYPE OUTPUT: Tony Gordon Ltd.

Printed in Canada

Introduction

Do you remember the last time you discovered something new, or met a new friend? Discovering new places, things, people or ideas is what makes life so much fun. Exploring the world around you is exciting, and exploring the past can be amazing.

I learned in school that Columbus was the first European to discover North America, but that's not true. My teachers also told me that the first Europeans to build settlements in North America were the French, in Canada, in 1608; but that's not true either.

Did my teachers lie to me? Of course not. The truth was not discovered until 1962 by Helge Ingstad and his wife, Anne Stine Ingstad.

When you set out to explore the past there are two ways to discover it. One is by reading; the other is by digging. Helge and Anne, who were Norwegians, had read exciting sagas written by the Vikings about the discovery of a new land. They believed the stories and, like the Vikings, they crossed the ocean to Canada. When they arrived in Newfoundland, Helge and Anne began to dig. Anne was an archaeologist. They dug and dug until, to everyone's surprise, they uncovered the ancient Viking settlement that they had read about.

So, thanks to Anne and Helge, we now know that the first Europeans to discover North America were the Vikings, in 998 A.D.

— about 500 years before Columbus. The Norsemen were also the first to build European settlements here in 1004 A.D.

Now it's your turn to discover the Vikings.

Back-Yard Archaeology

There are probably interesting artifacts in your back yard waiting to be discovered. You will be surprised at what you may find.

What You Need:
a bucket
an old collander or window screen
a garden trowel
an old paint brush
some string
eight sticks about 20 cm long
a notebook
a pencil

What To Do:

1. With your parents' help and permission, locate a site in your back yard to excavate. A good place might be behind the garage or toolshed.

2. Lay out a square one metre by one metre. Place a stick in the ground at each corner. Now divide the square into four equal parts by placing sticks halfway along each side. Tie string between the sticks to connect them and make a grid.

3. Draw a grid in your notebook and number the squares.

4. Begin digging in the first square. Carefully! Use the trowel to break up the top layer of soil. Now remove an inch or two of soil from the surface. Break it up with

your hands into the bucket. Look carefully at the cleared area. What do you see? If you see objects that you recognize, carefully brush the loose dirt away to expose them. Now stop!

5. Good archaeologists always record their finds in place before removing them. Draw the objects you see in the first square on the grid in your notebook. Now excavate the other squares.

6. After you have excavated and recorded the artifacts in all four squares, you may remove them.

7. Using the collander or screen, sift the dirt in the bucket to find any small objects you may have missed.

8. Finally, use the dirt to refill the hole. Archaeologists should always leave their sites as they found them.

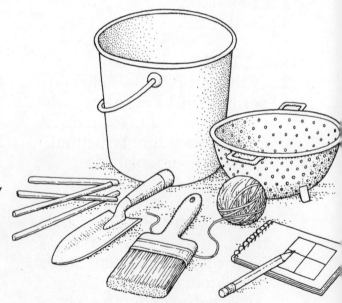

You may like to put identifying tags on your finds and start a museum on your shelf in your room.

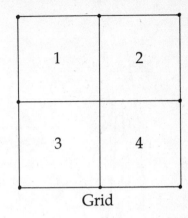

Grid

THINGS YOU MAY FIND

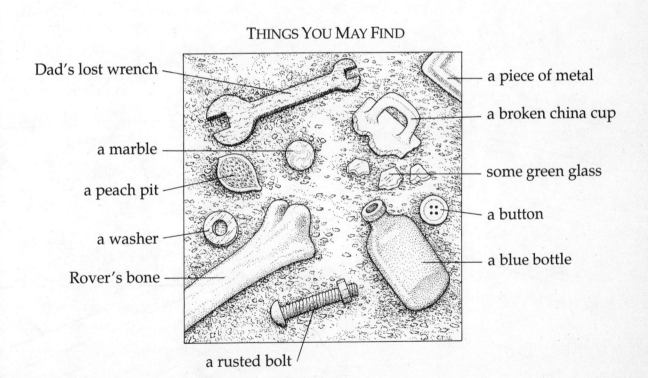

Dad's lost wrench

a marble

a peach pit

a washer

Rover's bone

a rusted bolt

a piece of metal

a broken china cup

some green glass

a button

a blue bottle

1 *Norsemen*

Vikings

Would you build your own boat and then sail it out on an endless, uncharted ocean, not knowing where you might end up? The Vikings did, because they loved adventure.

They had no idea what awaited them on the other side of the sea. It was equal to a spaceship full of astronauts blasting into outer space, not knowing where they might land, what dangers they could encounter or whether they would ever return.

The Norsemen were a rugged race of warriors and explorers. Their homeland was in northern Europe, a place similar to Canada in many ways. It had the same cold winters, tall forests and icy oceans. The cruel climate and rocky coastlines had caused the Vikings to become strong and aggressive.

The Viking villages were primitive and basic by our standards of living, but the Norse were an intelligent and ingenious people.

Vikings were good farmers as well as shipbuilders. They carved large, wooden figureheads on their wagons and ships. The young men would go to sea to trade goods and gather wealth so that they could later buy farmland on which to build a home.

Norsemen were natural sailors and, in their longships and *knarrs*, they set out to explore and conquer the world. It was common practice to raid and loot villages on the shores of England and Scotland. They would sometimes take prisoners and keep them as slaves.

The Viking Ship

The Viking ships were strongly built of *lapstrake* construction over a system of frames. They had large square sails and were guided by a steering board or rudder attached to the side of the ship by a leather thong.

stern —

steering board —

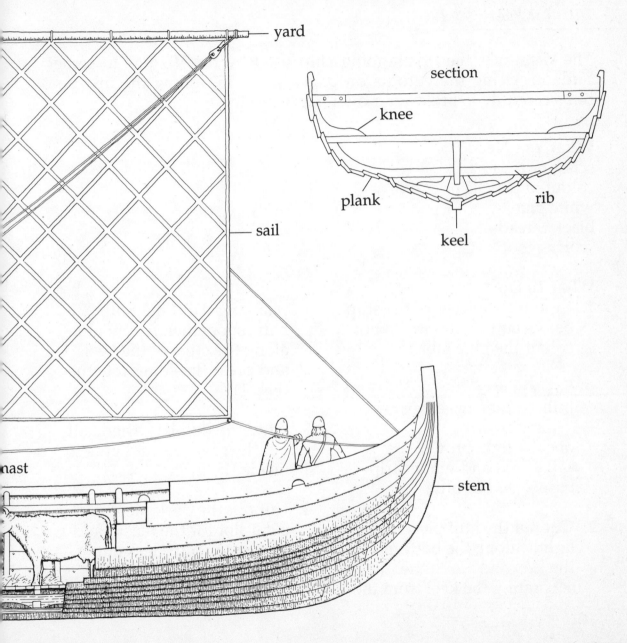

wind vane

yard

section

knee

sail

plank

rib

keel

mast

stem

9

Build a Viking Knarr

The *knarr* was the ocean-going ship used by the Vikings to settle Vinland. Using the cutouts on pages 13 to 15, follow the instructions carefully to build your own paper model.

What You Need:
scissors
coloured pencils or crayons
white glue
black thread
scoring tool

What To Do:
1. Colour the pieces of the ship before cutting it out. Do not colour the glue tabs.

   Suggestions:
   hull, rudder, mast, spar —
     dark brown
   deck — light brown
   sail — red and white stripes
   base — red or blue

2. Cut out the hull piece. Score lightly along the bottom of the keel and along the line separating the keel from the planking. Fold the hull halves together. Apply glue along the edge of the keel and press the edges together (Fig. 1).

3. After the hull has dried, cut out the rib piece and glue it inside the hull.

4. Cut out the deck piece and cut a slot for the mast. Fold the fore and aft decks up (Fig. 2). Apply glue to the deck tabs and top of the rib

piece and glue the deck in place.

5. Fold the mast piece (Fig. 3) and glue it together. After it has dried, cut out the mast, put a drop of glue at the bottom and insert it in the slot.

6. Fold the spar and glue it over the top of the sail. Glue the back of the spar to the top of the mast.

7. Cut out the rudder and glue it in position.

8. Use black thread to rig your ship as indicated in the drawing of the finished model.

9. Cut out and assemble the base (Fig. 4).

ASSEMBLY DIAGRAM

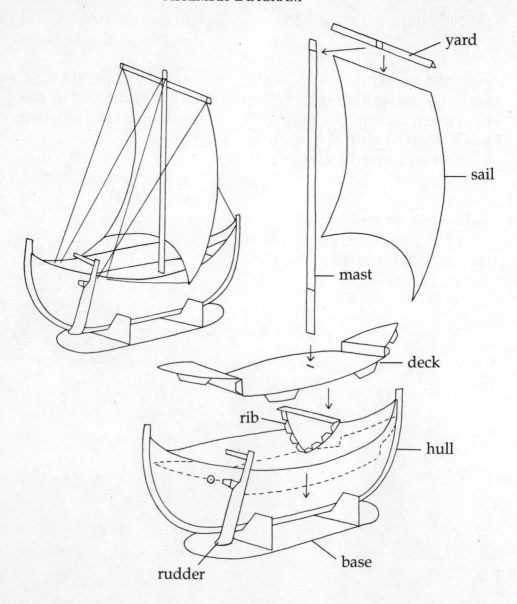

yard

sail

mast

deck

rib

hull

rudder

base

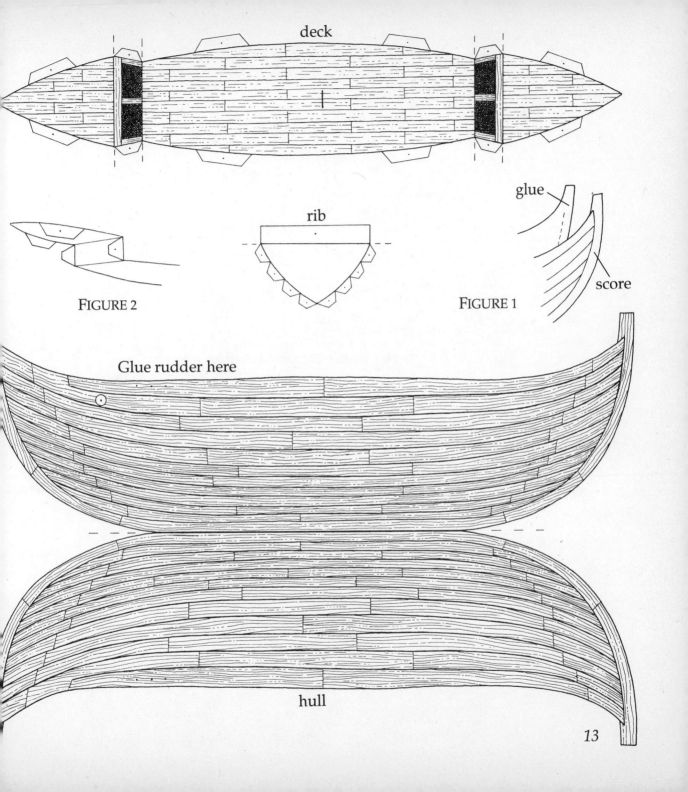

deck

rib

glue

score

FIGURE 2

FIGURE 1

Glue rudder here

hull

13

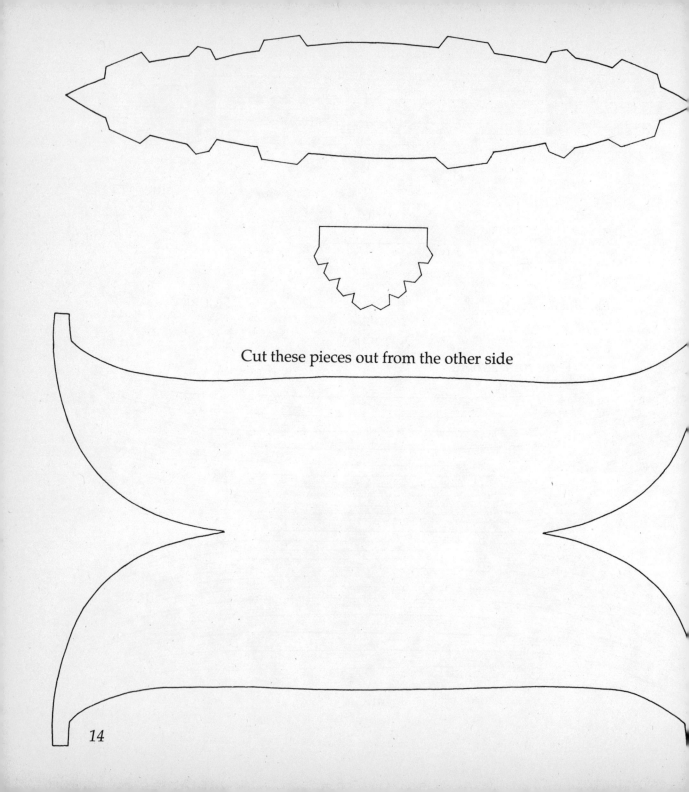

Cut these pieces out from the other side

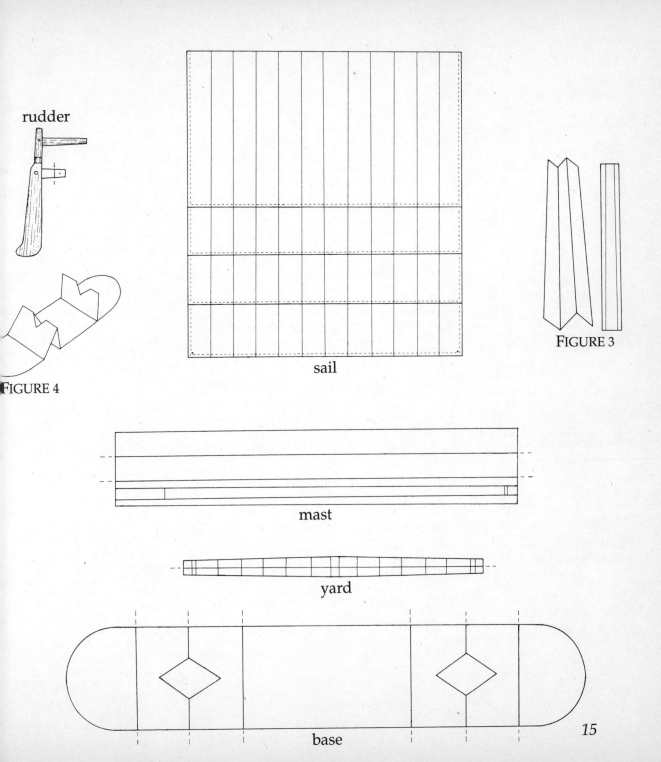

rudder

FIGURE 4

sail

FIGURE 3

mast

yard

base

15

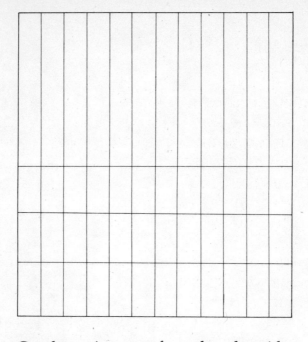

Cut these pieces out from the other side

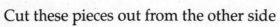

16

Port and Starboard

Many seafaring terms came from the Viking age. The term "starboard" for the right-hand side of a ship is derived from the fact that the "steering board" or rudder was always located on the right side of Viking ships. The ship was berthed with the dock on the left or "port" so that the steering board would not be damaged.

The term "stern" or rear part of a ship comes from the Old Norse *stjorn*, or rudder.

"Stem" — the curved timber at the front of a ship — comes from the Old Norse *stemma*.

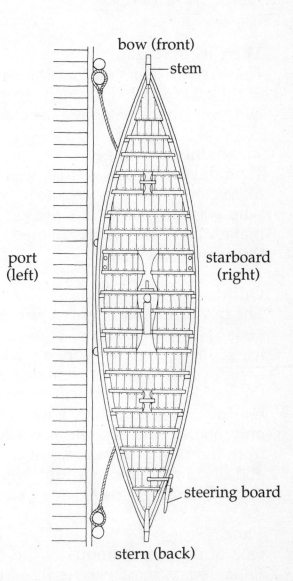

bow (front)

stem

port (left)

starboard (right)

steering board

stern (back)

The City of Asgard

The Vikings believed that the city of Asgard, which was the home of the gods, existed in the heavens. It had glittering roofs and golden towers that rose above the clouds.

The Rainbow Bridge

The rainbow bridge, Bifrost, was the only means of entering the city of Asgard from the outside world. It was guarded by Heimdall, who was famous for his horse called Gulltoppr that had a golden mane, and his horn named Gjallar which could be heard throughout the world.

Odin

The powerful and mighty Odin, the "Allfather," was the king of the gods. He was the god of war and hero of warriors. He was a fearsome figure who wore a golden helmet and had two large black ravens perched on his shoulder. Each day Odin sent the ravens into the outside world to see what was happening there. When they returned, they told him what they had seen and heard. Odin had only one eye because he had exchanged the other one for a drink from the Well of Wisdom. For this reason he was also known as the god of cunning and wisdom. His eight-legged horse, called Sleipnir, could fly through the air, and Odin liked to visit the earth in disguise.

Thor

One of the most famous of the Norse gods was the great warrior, Thor. Today, most people think of Thor as a comicbook character, but he was the Norse god of thunder. His hammer, "Mjolnir the Crusher," caused the lightning. Thor had to wear iron gauntlets because the hammer would return to his hand after striking his enemy. Thor was a friend of men and brought good luck in marriage. His day, *Thorsday*, which we call Thursday, was lucky for weddings. Although Thor was strong and brave, he was also known to be stupid and brutal at times.

Loki
The most evil of the Viking gods was Loki, the fire god or god of strife and destruction. He was the father of a monster in the shape of a wolf that was known as "Fenrir Wolf."

Balder
The most beautiful and kind of the Norse gods was the gentle Balder, whose name meant "shining." He was the son of Odin and Frigga and was the god of the sun. When he was born, his mother made all things swear that they would never harm him. But Loki, who was jealous of Balder, learned that the little mistletoe plant had been left out of the oath-taking. Because they knew that nothing could harm Balder, the other gods would childishly throw things at him in sport. The evil Loki persuaded Hodur, the blind god of autumn, Balder's twin brother, to join in the fun and gave him a sharp spear cut from a mistletoe branch. Guided by Loki, Hodur hurled it at Balder and killed him. With the death of Balder, beauty and innocence were gone from the world. Violence and evil increased and the "day of doom" arrived.

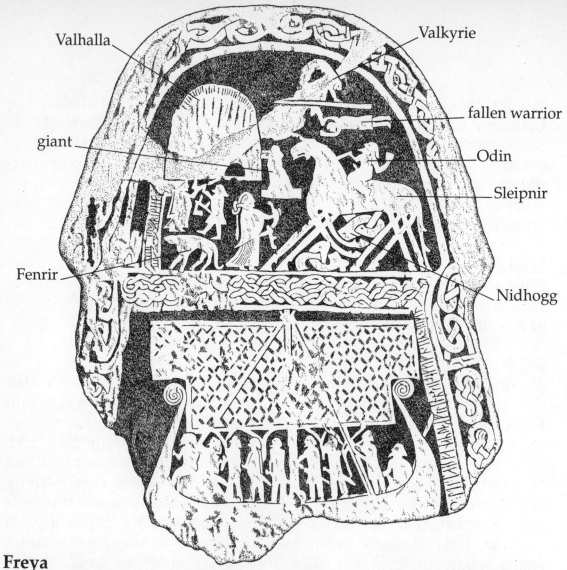

Valhalla

Valkyrie

giant

fallen warrior

Odin

Sleipnir

Fenrir

Nidhogg

Freya

Freya, whose chariot was drawn by two white cats, was the goddess of spring, love, marriage and fertility. Her symbol was the hawk and her glittering necklace, which had been made by the dwarfs, was the origin of many legends. Another of her treasures was her feather cloak, "Valhamr."

The Valkyrior

These woman warriors were mounted on horses, wore helmets and were armed with spears. Their name means "Choosers of the Slain" because the Norse believed that they were the messengers sent down to earth's battlefields to collect the bodies of the bravest heroes to join Odin's army in Valhalla. Their armour reflected a mysterious, flickering light that flashed across the northern skies, creating what we now call the Aurora Borealis, or Northern Lights.

Frigg

Frigg was the goddess most prayed to by Viking women, especially when they were about to have a baby. She was the wife of Odin and the only other person allowed to sit on his throne. She could predict the future and, on a golden distaff and spindle, spun yarn that was never used up, no matter how much was needed. It was believed that if a mortal woman worked very hard all day spinning yarn, Frigg would visit her as she slept and leave a present of her magic yarn.

Hel

Hel was the pale and ghost-like daughter of Loki. Odin sent her to rule the land of the dead, which was then called Hel, after the goddess. The walls of her huge hall were made of slithering serpents and on the roof was a pitch-black rooster. Hel's knife was called "Hunger," her table was called "Starvation" and her doorstep was known as "Pitfall." It was believed that all humans who died of sickness or old age were sent to Hel's kingdom.

Writing With Runes

The runic alphabet was invented by the ancient Scandinavian ancestors of the Vikings more than 2,000 years ago. The letters were made with straight lines that could be easily carved into wood or stone with a knife or chisel. The early runic alphabet had 24 letters. Later these were reduced to 16. The Vikings believed that some runes had magic powers and would bring them luck.

What You Need:
a pencil
a pad of paper

What To Do:
Printed on the opposite page is the 24-letter runic alphabet. Below each letter is its equivalent letter in our alphabet (the "Roman" alphabet). Study it carefully. How are they alike? How are they different?

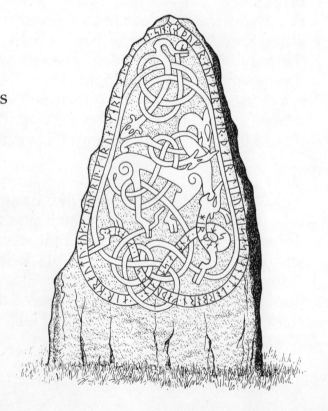

22

THE RUNIC ALPHABET

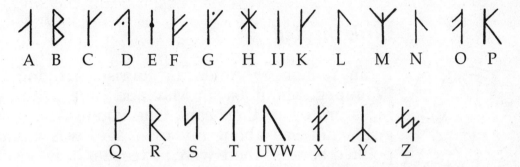

A B C D E F G H IJ K L M N O P

Q R S T UVW X Y Z

Below is a message written in runes. Translate it into English.
(The answer is on page 88.)

Now that you have translated the message above
write your own message in runes.

2 *Northern Neighbours*

Eirik the Red

I can remember American tourists arriving in Winnipeg, Manitoba, in May and June, with ski racks on top of their cars. One young American girl, who was about my own age, was disappointed because there were no teepees or igloos.

Do you sometimes become amused or annoyed because people in the U.S.A. know so little about Canada, or pay so little attention to us? The next time you feel irritated over the lack of knowledge the Americans have about Canada, stop and think about *your* northern neighbour, Greenland, and what you know about *it*.

In fact, the early history of Greenland was closely associated with the early history of Canada. It all began with a famous Viking leader known as "Eirik the Red."

Eirik the Red was strong, aggressive and adventurous. Like other Vikings before him, he sailed northwest to Iceland to seek his fortune and a new home.

There were no banks in Viking days. Eirik the Red carried with him an iron-bound, wooden sea chest, secured with a padlock. The Vikings used to sit on their sea chests when rowing their ships, thus keeping safe their share of the treasures gained in trading or looting.

Goods were bartered and traded, or purchased with a weight of gold or silver. Viking merchants carried a set of folding scales which they kept in a leather wallet or linen bag.

The Vikings also used to wear their wealth in the form of elaborate, decorated silver brooches and other jewellery. For example, the King would repay loyalty and courage with gold armrings or decorated swords.

Eirik the Red tried to settle in Iceland where other Vikings had made their homes, but he quarrelled with his neighbours. Because of the fighting, Eirik was declared an outlaw, and was forced to set sail to look for another home.

Eirik had heard of land to the west sighted by other Vikings, whose ships had been driven off course. He discovered and explored the new land. He named it "Greenland" because he wanted a good sounding name to encourage other settlers and traders. Eirik returned to Iceland and gathered a large group of people to colonize the new territory.

Thus, Eirik the Red became the founder of the first settlements in Greenland. Eirik had four children, three sons and a daughter. All of his children were to become involved with the early exploration and settlement of Canada.

Viking Art

This beautiful round brooch was found in a hoard of Viking silver on the island of Rugen in the Baltic Sea. Viking silversmiths made richly decorated jewellery with intricate interlacing patterns.

Making Change

The Vikings carried gold or silver coins to exchange for goods, but there were no coins of different values. If they needed to make change, they would simply *split* the coins into smaller segments with a chisel.

Lost at Sea

Twenty-five ships sailed with Eirik the Red to colonize Greenland, but only 14 arrived at their destination. The others were blown back by violent storms, or lost at sea.

Unisex Clothing

The earliest specimens of original clothing from the Middle Ages were discovered in Norse graves in the south of Greenland. The clothes of the men and women were exactly alike!

Christian Converts

In the year 1000 A.D., Christianity, which was spreading north from Europe, was adopted in Iceland. It was the wife of Eirik the Red, Thjodhild, who was the founder of the Christian Church in Greenland. She had a small church of turf and timber built near their farmstead and many others joined her there for prayers. Although his wife and children became Christians, Eirik refused to give up his beliefs in Odin and the other gods of Asgard. For this reason, Thjodhild refused to live with him after she was converted, and this angered Eirik the Red.

Viking Women

Viking women were as forceful and independent as the men. While the men were exploring or looting, the women managed the farms and were the ones who shaped the social structure.

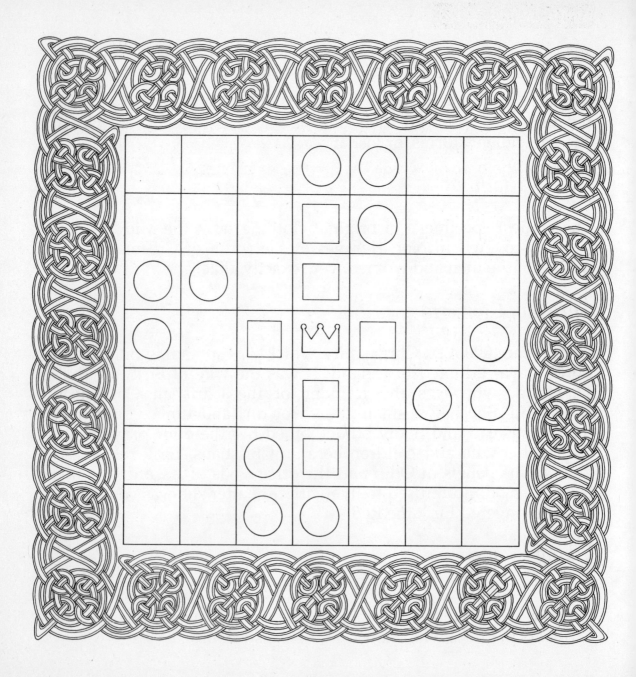

Play a Viking Board Game

Hnefatafl or "King's Table" is one of the games that Vikings played on the long cold Scandinavian nights. It is an ancient game known to have been played as early as 400 A.D. On the facing page is a board of the type on which the game was played.

What You Need:
You may use buttons or coloured stones for playing pieces. Use a larger one for the king.

Here are the rules for the game:

1. There are two sides. The king's team consists of the king and his guards. The king begins the game in the centre square (♛) surrounded by his guards on the squares marked (☐). The opposing team, the "usurpers," number twice the king's guard and begin the game on the squares marked (◯).

2. All players move as the rook moves in chess — as far vertically ↕ or horizontally ↔ as he wishes until blocked by another player.

3. Only the king can enter the king's square.

4. The object of the game for the king is to reach the outer edge of the board without being captured. The object of the opposing team is to capture the king.

5. Guards and usurpers are captured when they are surrounded by opposing pieces on two sides in a row.

6. The king is captured by being surrounded on four sides or three sides and the unoccupied centre square.

7. A piece may move between two opposing pieces without being captured. Capture must be initiated by the attacker.

8. The usurpers make the first move.

Odin's Raven

This is one of a pair of gilt bronze ravens that once decorated the harness or sword hilt of a Viking chieftain. It was found on the island of Gotland.

CHAPTER 3 *Getting Lost*

Bjarni Herjolfsson

When was the last time you were lost? Getting lost is a disturbing experience whether it is in the woods at night or in a large shopping mall. Often, the result is that you discover new places and meet new people. Sometimes the new people are friendly, but they can also be dangerous.

It was not unusual for Viking ships to get lost. The Norse sailors did not have magnetic compasses or sextants. Before setting out on a voyage, a Viking would first make a *husnotra*, which was a primitive compass that could determine latitude. This stick-like instrument enabled the Norse sailors to hold a direction. Other basic navigational aids (such as the sun, the moon, the North Star, sea birds or the glow given off by land on the horizon) would also assist them, but frequently they would be blown off course or lost at sea.

When Eirik the Red settled in Greenland, he had a partner, Herjolf Herjolfsson, who had a son named Bjarni Herjolfsson. When Bjarni set sail for Greenland to visit his father, he became lost at sea. Eventually his ship was blown far to the west where he discovered a strange new continent. Using his *husnotra*, Bjarni followed the coastline of the unknown territory north and east until he found his way back to Greenland. The mysterious, uncharted land which Bjarni accidentally discovered was the east coast of North America. So, it was Bjarni Herjolfsson who discovered America, not Christopher Columbus.

Norse Navigation

How were the Vikings, who did not possess the magnetic compass or other modern navigational instruments, able to cross the open seas and arrive at their destinations? They learned to sail across lines of latitude by taking measurements from the noon-day sun during the day and the North Star at night.

The height of the sun above the horizon at noon along any line of latitude is the same all the way around the world on the same day of the year. Before leaving his home in Norway, the Viking seafarer would make a *husnotra* — a stick or perhaps a set of sticks — with the position of the noon sun marked on them with notches. Later, when he was far out of sight of land he could take a measurement with the given stick for that day and determine how far north or south of his home port he was.

• SOMETHING TO DO •

Finding your Latitude

What You Need:
a globe

What To Do:
On the next page is a diagram and chart demonstrating lines of latitude. Look at the globe and find the lines of latitude.

Along what line of latitude do you live? What other places around the world lay along the same line?

LINES OF LATITUDE

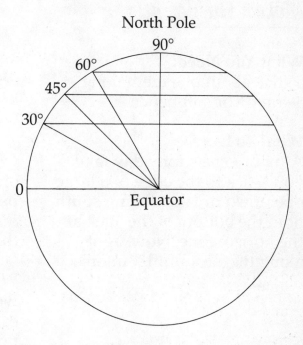

Places around the world that lay along the same lines of latitude.

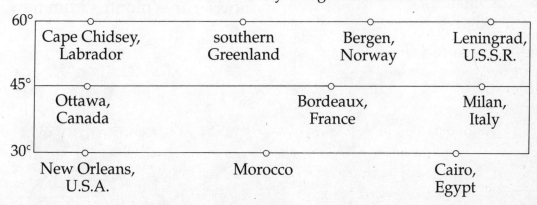

60°	Cape Chidsey, Labrador	southern Greenland	Bergen, Norway	Leningrad, U.S.S.R.
45°	Ottawa, Canada		Bordeaux, France	Milan, Italy
30°	New Orleans, U.S.A.	Morocco		Cairo, Egypt

Make a Husnotra

What You Need:
a stick about one metre long
a crayon or soft pencil

What To Do:
At noon on a sunny day take your stick to the edge of a large open field or lake. Facing south, hold the bottom of the stick at the horizon line. Now sight along the stick until it intersects with the sun. Mark the position on your *husnotra* with the pencil. *Caution*: Do not stare directly at the sun for more than a moment.

What would happen if you were a thousand miles directly east or west of your present position? What would be the position of the sun on your stick exactly one year from now? Three months from now?

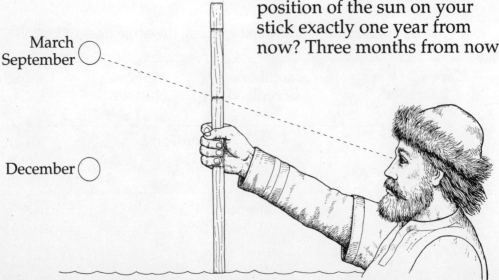

June
mid-day Sun ◯

March
September ◯

December ◯

Find the North Star

The North Star remains over the North Pole on every night of the year. The other stars and constellations appear to revolve around it.

What You Need:
a clear starry night

What To Do:
Locate the Big Dipper. Now using the two pointers find the North Star. When facing the North Star, which direction is south? east? west?

The Vikings also used migrating birds, ocean currents and fish to aid them in navigating.

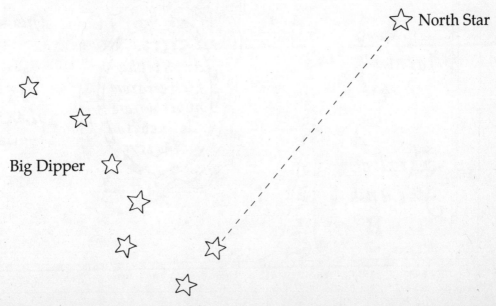

North Star

Big Dipper

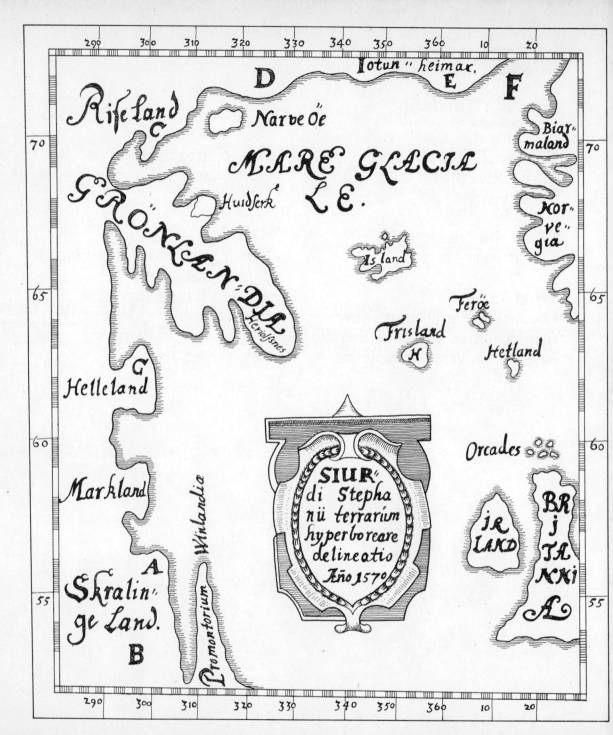

Iotun heimar.

D   E   F

Rise Land   C   Narve Öe

Biar
maland

MARE GLACIA
LE.

Huidserk

Nor
ve
gia

GRÖNLANDIA

Is land

Heriolfsnes

Feröe

Frisland

Hetland

H

G
Helleland

Orcades

Markland

SIUR
di Stepha
nü terrarum
hyperboreare
delineatio
Año 1570

Winlandia

IR
LAND

BR
j
TA
NNi
A

A
Skralin
ge Land.

Promontorium

B

The Skaholt Map

On the opposite page is a reproduction of the North Atlantic map drawn in 1590 by Sigurdur Stefansson. It includes Great Britain and Norway to the east, the Arctic Ocean in the north and Greenland, Helleland (Baffin Island), Markland (Labrador), Skraelinge Land (Red Indian Land) and Promontorium Winlandiae (Vinland Promontory) to the west. Stefannson attached the following notes to his map:

(A) These people [*skraelings*] are dried up just as much by the summer heat as the winter cold.
(B) South of Skraelinge Land lies Vinland, called "The Good" because of the fertility of the land and its abundant produce. From more recent historian accounts, I calculate that it is not connected to the mainland but is an island, separated from America either by a strait or a bay.

The Island that Disappeared

The Vikings and other early sailors used to make maps of their travels, such as the one shown here. On all of the early maps, a small island appeared in the northern seas. The name of the island was *Frisland*, but today there is no trace of it. It has *disappeared*!

4 *Exploring*

Leif the Lucky

Whenever you discover something new or different, there is always a strong instinct to explore or investigate it. When Bjarni reported his discovery to the other Vikings, they were not pleased with him. They believed that Bjarni should have taken the time to land and explore the new continent, instead of being in a rush to find his way back home.

There was one young Viking who was extremely excited about the new land. His name was Leif Eiriksson and he was the oldest son of Eirik the Red. Leif went to visit Bjarni, and after listening to the stories about the new land to the west, Leif purchased Bjarni's ship and collected a crew of 35 sailors.

As he set out to investigate the uncharted seas to the west, Leif first found a barren coastline where he cast anchor, lowered a small boat and landed. There was no grass or vegetation, only great glaciers that resembled a flat slab of rock. Leif named the country *Helluland*, which meant "Slab Island" or "Flatstone Land." Today we call it Baffin Island.

Leif then proceeded farther west and south where he sighted a second land. Again he went ashore to investigate and found thick forests and sandy beaches. Leif named this place *Markland*, which meant "Forest Land." Today it is known as the Labrador coast.

Leif continued south until he came to another land mass. Here his men took their hammocks ashore and built stone and turf enclosures, using awnings as roofs. The rivers were full of salmon and the land was rich with berries and vines. Leif named the place *Vinland*, which meant "Wine Land." Today it is Newfoundland, a province of Canada. Loading his ship with timber and wild wine-berries, Leif returned to Greenland.

On the trip home, Leif sighted a group of 15 people stranded on a reef where they had been shipwrecked. He rescued them, and from that time Leif became known as "Leif the Lucky."

Therefore, it was Leif the Lucky who was the first European to explore the continent of America.

Write a Saga

The Vikings told stories, called sagas, about their country, their friends, their families and themselves.

What You Need:
a pencil/or a pen/or a typewriter/or
a computer with a word-processing kit
some paper
lots of imagination

What To Do:

A. The Personal Saga

1. Viking sagas were true experiences. Think about something that happened to you recently. It doesn't have to be anything unusual, just something involving you, your friends or your family.

    Examples:
    a trip to the mall
    a personal accomplishment
    a sports event
    a walk to school
    a classroom experience
    sleeping over at a friend's house

2. Write a brief outline of the event.

    Example: Last Tuesday I left the house to go to school. On the way I met my two friends, Andre and Nancy. We walked together until we saw George . . .

3. Viking sagas were written to entertain the readers. Add some exaggeration to your saga. Rewrite each sentence in an effort to capture the imagination of the readers. Don't be shy. Brag about your talents!

Example: It was the coldest winter day of my entire life but, wrapped in protective clothing, I bravely forced myself out of the door and headed for school. Within a few minutes the tip of my nose was frozen hard as an ice cube and my breath was turning to icicles the second it left my mouth.

4. The Vikings invented names that described people's appearance, personality, or accomplishments.

   Examples of authentic Norse names:
   Thorhall the Hunter
   Thord Horse-Head
   Ketil Flat-Nose
   Aud the Deep-Minded
   Lady Ingigerd the Powerful
   Thorstein the Unjust

   Invent Viking names for anyone who is in your saga and also one for yourself.

Examples
Andre the Brain Child
Nancy the Bold
George the Giant
Betty Big-Foot
Mark the Money-Lender

5. The Vikings believed in a world of mythology and mystery. They often added something supernatural to their sagas. You should do the same.

   Examples:
   Because of my strange dream, I knew that Tuesday would not be a normal day.

   Just before we turned the corner, I felt an eerie sensation that we were walking into danger.

   Andre's eyes flashed ferociously, an animal-like growl came from deep in his throat and his front teeth grew into fangs.

I felt an icy finger on my shoulder and turned to find myself face to face with the Snow Monster.

6. Make the last sentence in your saga an interesting one that sums up the experience.

Examples:
I rushed desperately through the schoolhouse door and slammed it shut behind me. I had never been so happy to arrive at school.

Andre, Nancy and I never talk about that day; it is an unspoken agreement.

We all laughed happily, especially George the Giant.

7. Finally, decide on a title for your saga.

Examples:
The Saga of George
   the Giant
The Saga of Truth and
   Temptation
The Main Street Saga
The Saga of Snowy Tuesday

B. The Ancestral Saga
The Viking sagas were told orally and passed down from one generation to another. Often the written version did not appear until hundreds of years after the events. Think of a story you have heard from your parents, your grandparents or older people in your community. If you can't remember one, ask an older person to tell you about one of the following:
— the way things used to be
— how you came to live here
— the most unusual person in your family
— a well-known leader in the history of your city or country
Now follow the same seven steps outlined in "The Personal Saga."

C. The Back-Yard Saga
   Choose one of the things you
   found when you became a
   "Back-Yard Archaeologist."
   Invent a saga that explains
   how the object might have
   gotten into your back yard.
   Use the same seven steps outlined in "The Personal Saga."

The Bad Omen

Eirik the Red, who was the founder of Greenland, had three sons and a daughter. All four of his children sailed to Vinland in search of wealth and fame. However, Eirik never made the voyage.

When Leif was preparing to leave for Vinland, he had persuaded his father to join him, but a bizzare accident prevented Eirik from making the expedition. He fell from his horse on the way to the ship. The Vikings, who were very superstitious, believed that such an accident was a "bad omen," so Eirik remained in Greenland.

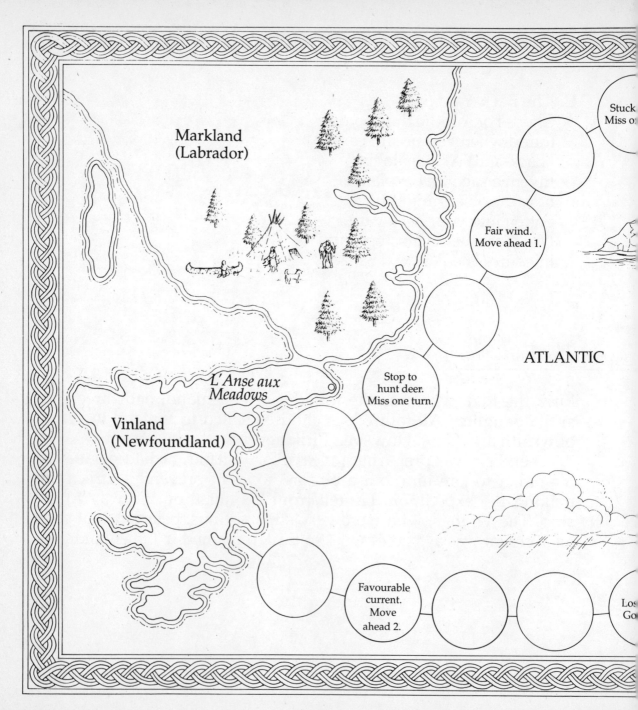

Markland
(Labrador)

L'Anse aux
Meadows

Vinland
(Newfoundland)

ATLANTIC

Stuck
Miss o

Fair wind.
Move ahead 1.

Stop to
hunt deer.
Miss one turn.

Favourable
current.
Move
ahead 2.

Los
Go

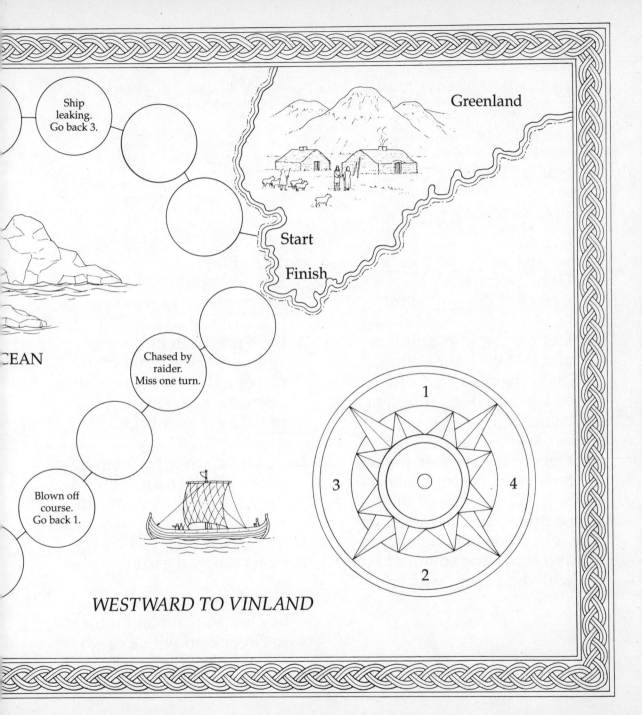

Ship
leaking.
Go back 3.

Greenland

Start

Finish

CEAN

Chased by
raider.
Miss one turn.

Blown off
course.
Go back 1.

1

3   4

2

WESTWARD TO VINLAND

Play a Game of Viking Adventure — Westward to Vinland

What You Need:
scissors
a small piece of thin cardboard
glue
a paper fastener

What To Do:
1. Glue the paper on page 47 to a piece of the cardboard.

2. Cut out the ship counters and fold back the bottoms to make them stand. Colour the sail of each one a different colour.

3. Cut out the spinner, make a hole in the centre. Make a hole in the centre of the compass circle at the lower right of the playing board and attach the spinner to it with the paper fastener.

How To Play:
1. Spin the spinner to see which player moves first.

2. Each player in turn spins and moves the number of places indicated. Follow the instruction on any of the specially marked circles.

3. As you approach Vinland, you must spin the correct number to land directly on Vinland. You may spin only once each turn (more than one player may occupy the same circle).

4. The first player whose ship reaches Vinland and returns to Greenland with a cargo is the winner. Good luck!

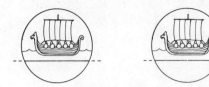

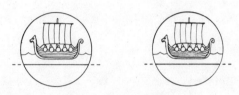

Cut out the ships. Fold back the bases and colour each sail a different colour.

Cut out the centre of the spinner and attach it to the compass circle with a paper fastener.

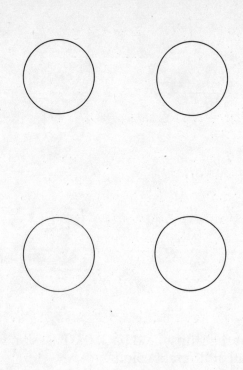

48

5

Starting a Fight

Thorvald Eiriksson

Have you ever been involved in a fight? Most people try to avoid fighting because it is unfriendly and dangerous. When you start a fight, you never know how it will end.

The Vikings were warriors who were always ready to attack and plunder. When they came to Vinland, they came with their swords drawn, ready to fight.

When Leif the Lucky returned to Greenland with a rich cargo, he became famous. His younger brother, Thorvald Eiriksson, wanted to explore the new lands more thoroughly. He borrowed his brother's ship, gathered a crew of 30 men and sailed west.

When they arrived at the houses that Leif had built in Vinland, they settled down for the winter, living on the fish and game in the area. In the summer they set out to explore the new country.

On one expedition, they saw three "skin boats" on a sandy beach. There were three men under each boat, so Thorvald divided his forces and captured the strange natives, but one escaped.

The Vikings killed the eight *skraelings*, or Indians, whom they captured and started back to their ship. But the native who had escaped had gone for help. Suddenly, a large force of natives in skin boats descended upon them. After some ferocious fighting, the Indians retreated.

There was only one Viking who was killed in the encounter. Thorvald, who had started the fight, died of an arrow wound. His men buried him in the strange new land where he had lost his life.

Thus, it was the second son of Eirik the Red, Thorvald Eiriksson, who was the first European to be killed by North American natives.

One-Legged Creatures

The Vikings had many superstitious beliefs and one of them was in the mythical creatures known as "unipeds." These small, dark men had only one leg and possessed magical powers. The myths of unipeds were usually associated with creatures in Africa.

One version of the death of Thorvald describes how he met a uniped on the shores of Vinland and it shot him with an arrow. One of the Vikings made up the following poem about the incident.

Yes, it's true
That our men chased
A Uniped
Down to the sea;
The weird creature
Ran like the wind
Over rough ground;
Hear that, Karlsefni.

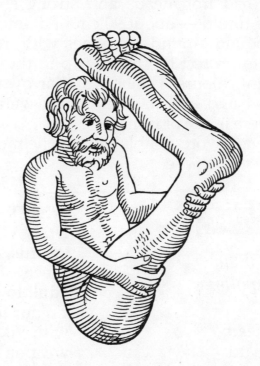

Viking Weapons

The principal weapons of a Viking warrior were his sword, axe and spear. The sword was the most popular and was often given a name like "skull-splitter" or "long and sharp." Their hilts were often decorated with inlays of gold and silver wire. A prized sword was often passed from father to son.

Although the axe had fallen out of favour in the rest of Europe, it remained a popular weapon with the Vikings. The spears used by the Vikings had iron heads and strong shafts made of ash. The shields were round — about 90 cm in diameter. They were made of wood and bound around the edges with iron. In the centre was a round boss to protect the hand grip in the back. The shields were painted bright colours. The bow and arrow was used by Vikings to fight on land and at sea. Their bows were of wood and the arrowheads were made of iron.

Most Vikings wore simple conical helmets. Some had *nasals* in front to protect the nose.

• SOMETHING TO DO •

Make your own Viking weapons

What You Need:
some cardboard
a utility knife
crayons

What To Do:
Draw Viking weapons like swords, axes and shields on sheets of cardboard. Ask an adult to cut them out for you. Colour them and decorate them with Viking designs. Give your weapons names and write them in runes. Display your weapons on the wall of your room.

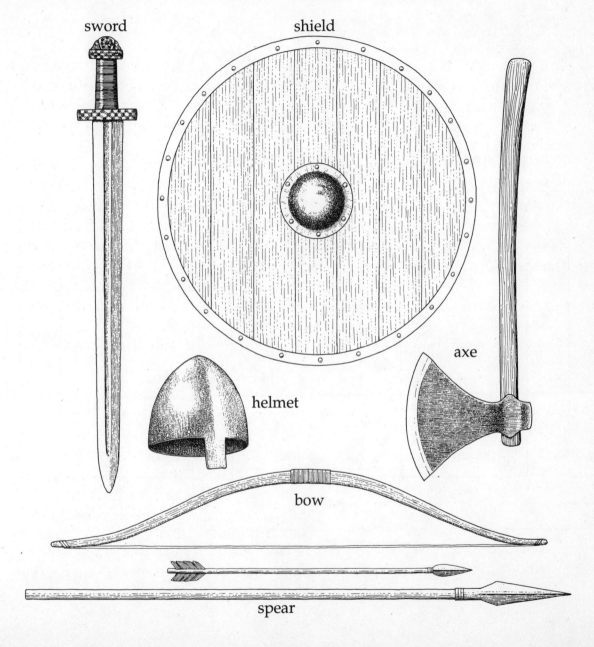

sword

shield

axe

helmet

bow

spear

53

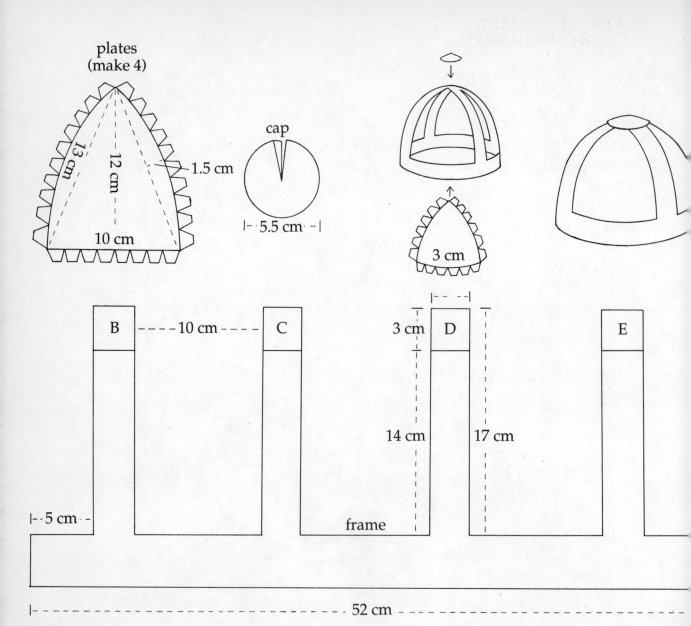

plates
(make 4)

13 cm

12 cm

1.5 cm

10 cm

cap

|- 5.5 cm -|

3 cm

B ---- 10 cm ---- C

3 cm D

E

14 cm

17 cm

|- 5 cm -|

frame

|- --- --- --- --- --- 52 cm --- --- --- --- -|

Make a Viking Helmet

What You Need:
a piece of construction paper, 60 cm x 42 cm
a pencil
a ruler
scissors
glue

What To Do:

1. Following the plan on the opposite page, lay out the pieces on a piece of construction paper (remember to make four "plate" pieces). You may wish to decorate your helmet with your name in runes or with Viking designs before assembling.

2. Cut out the pieces for the frame. Glue tab A to the other end of the band. Glue tabs B, C, D and E over each other at the top.

3. After the frame has dried, cut out the four plates. Score along the edges of the tabs and glue them to the inside of the frame.

4. Cut out and assemble the cap and glue it to the top of the frame.

CHAPTER 6 *The Youngest Son*

Thorstein Eiriksson

Is there someone in your life whom you look up to and try to imitate? Most of us copy the behaviour of our friends and family members, especially if they are older than we are.

The third son of Eirik the Red was Thorstein Eiriksson. Like many little brothers, Thorstein was anxious to follow in the footsteps of his older brothers, Leif and Thorvald.

One day he announced his intention to travel to Vinland. Thorstein wanted to explore the new territories and carry out a personal quest. His goal was to bring back to Greenland the body of his brother, Thorvald, who had been killed by natives. He picked a crew of 25 strong sailors and set out in the same ship that had carried his brothers before him. Travelling with him was his beautiful young wife, Gudrid.

The voyage was doomed from the start. Throughout the summer, their ship was battered by fierce storms and they were unable to reach Vinland.

One week before winter, they sighted land at Lysufjord in the western settlement of Greenland. They landed and prepared to remain there for the winter. Thorstein and Gudrid were invited to stay at the home of another Viking who was also named Thorstein, "Thorstein the Black."

During the winter a deadly disease broke out in the settlement. It killed Thorstein Eiriksson and most of his men. In the spring, the young widow (who was said to be magically gifted) sailed back to Eiriksfjord, the home of her father-in-law, Eirik the Red, carrying a cargo of bodies.

Ironically, it was Thorstein's own corpse that was brought back to Greenland for Christian burial, not the body of his brother, Thorvald, as he had imagined.

Women's Lib

Under Icelandic law in the year 1000 A.D., a woman had equal rights in marriage. She could also demand a divorce and receive half her husband's estate if she could prove her claim.

The Talking Dead

It is written in the sagas that after Thorstein had died of disease, his body sat upright and called out three times: "Where is Gudrid?" The corpse of Thorstein then predicted that Gudrid would be remarried to a stranger from Iceland, and that the marriage would be, "great and vigorous, bright and excellent, sweet and fragrant."

The Viking Nun

Gudrid survived all her husbands and undertook a pilgrimage to Rome. When she returned to Iceland, she was ordained a nun and lived out the rest of her life in a newly constructed church.

Winter Sports

In the winter, Viking boys and girls skated on the frozen lakes and rivers. Their skates were not made of metal but from the shin bones of animals. The bottoms of the bones were flattened and holes were made at the front and back for laces to tie them to their feet.

This skate was found at Birka, a Viking trading centre in Sweden.

Cross-country skiing was also a popular sport as well as a means of winter transportation.

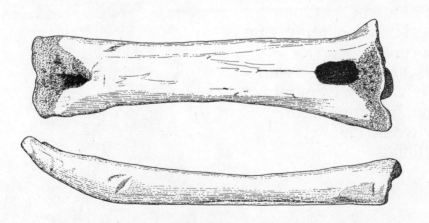

Dice

Games of chance were popular with Vikings. These dice made of bone were found in the excavation of the Viking settlement at York (Yorvik) in England.

Chess

Chess had been introduced to Europe from the East. By the Viking period it was played throughout Scandinavia. A set of chess pieces made of walrus ivory has been found on the Island of Lewis in the Outer Hebrides. This piece represents a twelfth-century warrior known as a *berserker*. It is said that these warriors went into such a frenzy before a battle that they would chew the edges of their shields.

7 Seeking a Home

CHAPTER

Gudrid and Karlsefni

The place where you live today is your home, but someday you will probably find a new home. You may travel to another city or even another country in search of it.

One day, a Viking ship arrived from Iceland at the home of Eirik the Red in Greenland. Its captain was a handsome and wealthy young man named Thorfinn Karlsefni.

Living with Eirik was his beautiful and intelligent daughter-in-law, Gudrid. She was the young widow who had been married to Eirik's youngest son, Thorstein, until he died suddenly from disease.

When Karlsefni saw the attractive Gudrid, he immediately fell in love. Because she was living in the home of her father-in-law, Karlsefni asked Eirik if he could propose marriage to her. Eirik agreed, and so did Gudrid.

From Gudrid, Karlsefni heard intriguing stories about Vinland, and they decided to make it their permanent home. They loaded four ships with supplies and livestock, and with 160 men and women they headed for Vinland.

When they arrived in Vinland in 1004 A.D., they built a settlement which they called Straumfjord (today it is called L'Anse aux Meadows). This is the place that archaeologists Helge and Anne Ingstad believe they discovered in Newfoundland in 1962.

A Viking home was very different from yours. If they needed a fire for cooking or warmth, they had no matches. They would make tinder (a small quantity of dry leaves and grass), then strike a piece of iron against a flint which would produce a hot spark that would fall on the tinder and begin to burn.

The houses at L'Anse aux Meadows had turf walls and wooden ceilings with a smoke hole over top of the fire. Many of the tools and household utensils were carved from wood: spades, axe handles, casks, buckets, bowls, cups and combs.

The Vikings used metal to make horseshoes, keys, locks, knives, swords and axes. The Indians tried to exchange furs for weapons, but Karlsefni forbade his people from giving them weapons. He told them to trade only milk and red cloth. The natives had never tasted milk nor seen coloured cloth; they were eager to trade.

The Vikings knew how to use wool to create different patterns in cloth. They would first comb the wool with wood combs that had iron teeth. Next, the wool would be spun by using a spindle with weights hanging from it (a spindle whorl).

Karlsefni's settlers lived peaceably with the natives for three years and many of the Vikings married native women. But one day trouble broke out. An Indian was caught trying to steal a weapon, and one of the Vikings killed him. The natives returned with a large army and a bloody battle broke out. The Vikings were beaten back to their ships and forced to abandon their settlement.

Karlsefni hated to admit defeat, but he decided that the natives were too warlike to permit a Norse colony. Sadly, he sailed back to Greenland. The first attempt by Europeans to make North America their home ended in failure.

Bronze Ringed Pin

This cloak pin was found at L'Anse aux Meadows. These pins, which served much the same purpose as our safety pins, were very popular. They have also been found at Viking settlements in England, Scotland, Ireland and Iceland.

Stone Spindle Whorl

The finding of a spindle whorl at L'Anse aux Meadows indicates that the spinning of wool into yarn took place there. This is also evidence that women were present in the settlement.

THE VIKING VILLAGE AT L'ANSE AUX MEADOWS CA. 1004

65

The Viking Settlement at L'Anse aux Meadows

In the new colony the settlers carried out the normal occupations of the day. The stream now known as Black Duck Brook provided fresh water. Nearby forests would have supplied timber for building houses and repairing the boats and ships. There was plenty of fine grass for the livestock and the nearby bay was filled with fish which were caught and hung on racks to dry. The smith smelted iron ore from local bogs to be made into new tools and nails.

The Plan of the Settlement

The Ingstad team and others that followed carried out extensive excavations of the area around L'Anse aux Meadows. They discovered the remains of three large houses and outbuildings of types that were known in Iceland and Greenland. On the west side of Black Duck Brook they discovered the remains of a smithy. Along the shore of Epaves Bay recent excavations have revealed buildings that appear to be boat sheds. Parks Canada has reconstructed several buildings near the original site so that visitors may better understand how the Viking settlers lived.

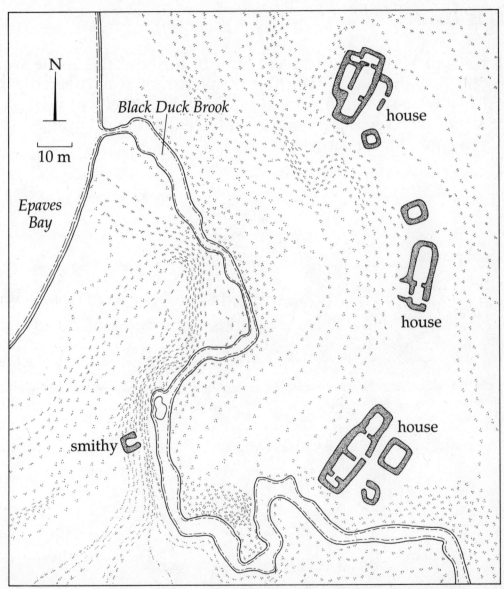

N

10 m

Epaves Bay

Black Duck Brook

house

house

house

smithy

THE PLAN OF THE VIKING SETTLEMENT AT L'ANSE AUX MEADOWS

Viking House

The walls of Viking houses were built of turf and the inside walls were lined with wood. Even the planked roof was covered with turf. They were so well insulated that very little fuel was needed to heat them. Wood was very scarce in Greenland and voyages were made to Labrador for cargoes of timber.

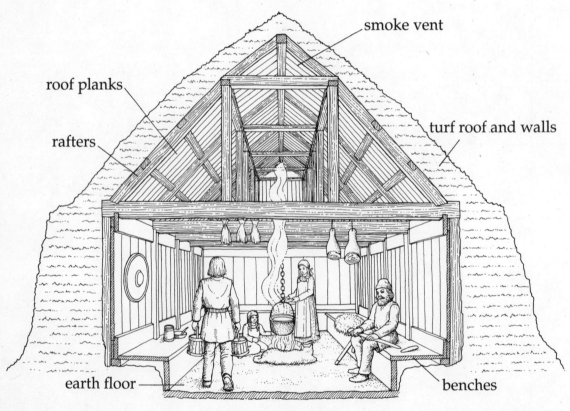

VIKING HOUSE

Build a Viking House

The Viking houses were built of stone and sod. Even the wooden roof planks were covered in sod. Follow the instructions carefully to build your own Viking house.

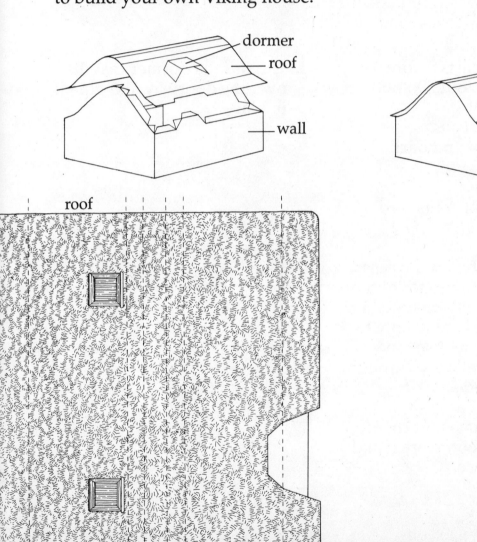

dormer

roof

wall

roof

What You Need:
scissors
crayons or coloured pencils
white glue
scoring tool

What To Do:
1. Colour the parts before cutting them out. Do not colour the tabs.
   Colour suggestions:
   walls — light and dark brown
   roof — green
   door and roof vents — dark brown

2. Cut out the two wall pieces. Score along the edges of the tabs and glue them together. *Caution*: Apply glue only to the tabs. Do not use too much or it will seep through the paper and spoil it.

3. After the walls have dried, cut out the roof, score it and glue it in place.

4. Cut out the dormer that fits over the doorway and glue it in place.

Cut out other side

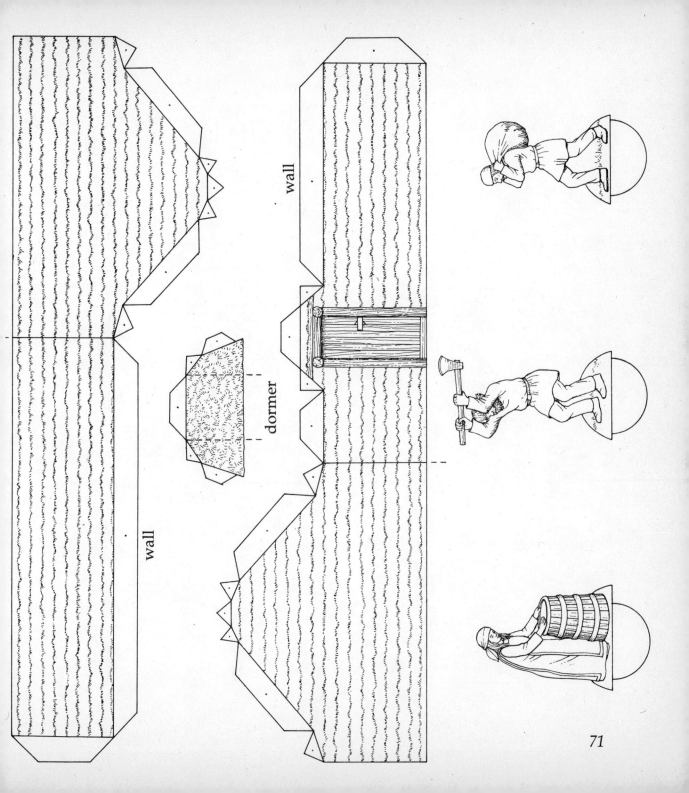

wall

wall

dormer

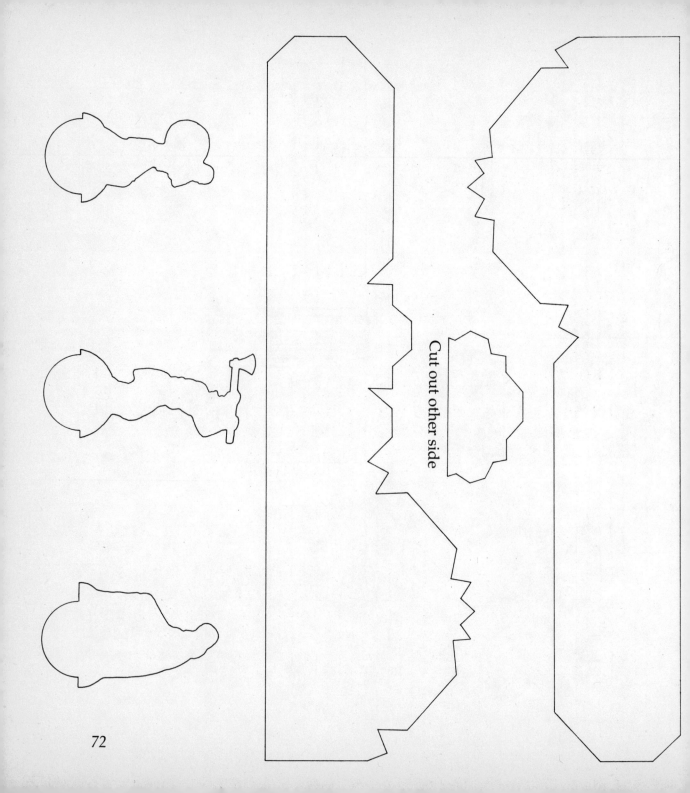

Cut out other side

Snorri

The first white child was born in North America in 1004 A.D. His name was Snorri and he was the son of Karlsefni and his wife, Gudrid.

Scottish Slaves

When Karlsefni set out to colonize Vinland, Leif the Lucky gave him a present of two Scottish slaves who could run faster than a deer. The man was called Haki and the woman was called Hekja. When they reached North America, Karlsefni put the two Scots ashore and told them to run southward to explore the country and return within three days. It has been suggested that the Scots were used as decoys to discover whether the natives were dangerous. They both wore a garment called a *bjafal*, which had a hood at the top and was open at the sides. It had no sleeves and was fastened between the legs with a loop and a button. That was all they wore.

Haki and Hekja returned safely three days later with samples of grapes and wild wheat.

The Charging Bull

One day as Karlsefni and his people were trading peacefully with a group of natives, a bull that belonged to Karlsefni came charging out of the woods bellowing loudly. The Indians had never seen such a creature before and ran terrified to their skin boats. Three weeks later a huge army of *skraelings* returned waving rattle-sticks and howling ferociously. A bloody battle then took place.

74

CHAPTER 8 *Native People*

Skraelings

When the Vikings arrived in North America, they encountered two main groups of native people. Usually the Norse referred to all natives as *skraelings*, which was an insulting term that meant "wretch."

Try to imagine what thoughts ran through the minds of the North American Indians when they first encountered the Vikings. The Indians still used weapons and tools made of wood and stone; the Vikings had metal swords and tools. The natives wore animal skins; the Norse dressed in colourful woven fabrics. The Indians had to hunt and fish for food; the Vikings relied on farming and farm animals for their food. The natives lived in tents made of animal skins; the Norse built houses of stone and wood. The Indians travelled in small canoes made from the bark of trees or animal skins; the Vikings built large ocean-going ships.

In the north, on Baffin Island (Helluland), the Vikings met the Inuit. These natives are commonly called "Eskimos," but this is an insulting name given to them by southern natives, meaning "eaters of raw flesh."

Along the coast of Newfoundland (Vinland), the Vikings discovered the mysterious Beothuk Indians. Although these native people were usually friendly and eager to trade, the encounters between natives and Norsemen often resulted in fighting and bloodshed. It was almost always the Vikings who caused the fight, although the natives were very capable of defending themselves.

The Boethuks were a proud and strong race. It was their custom to stain their faces red with berries, thus giving rise in later centuries to the term "red-skins," which became a general label for all North American Indians.

Hundreds of years after they had stood up to the Vikings and discouraged them from settling in North America, the fierce Beothuk warriors fought with French and English settlers. The fate of the proud tribe is the shame of the white settlers of Newfoundland, who placed a bounty on their heads. The entire tribe, including women and children, was eventually killed like animals by bounty hunters.

White Indians

When the Vikings arrived in Vinland, they encountered the mysterious Indian tribe known as the Beothuks. Some of the Beothuks had blue eyes and white skin. They were also taller than the other Indians.

Because some Vikings married native women, it is understandable how later generations of white Indians could have developed after the Vikings returned home. But, how would you explain the white Indians who met the Vikings when they arrived? Maybe the white Indians were descendants of Vikings or other sailors whose ships were lost at sea and blown to the east coast of Canada years before Karlsefni arrived.

White Men's Land

From captured natives, the Vikings learned of a place called *Hvitramannaland* (literally "White Men's Land"), where the people dressed in white clothing, carried poles with patches of coloured cloth attached and uttered loud cries.

The concept of a country of white people (Albania-land) is found in Icelandic as well as Irish legends where it is called *Tir na bhFear bhFionn* (Land of the White Men). It was thought to lie six days' sail west of Ireland. Could this mysterious White Men's Land have been the lost continent of Atlantis?

Exploding Globes

During one battle with the *skraelings*, the Vikings were terrified and confused when the natives used catapults to fling weird, exploding globes. The large spheres were dark blue in colour and after they flew over the heads of the Norsemen, they made a loud din as they struck the ground. The Vikings fled in panic and disorder. This device has been compared with the *ballista* used by Algonquin Indians, and was probably made of inflated seal bladders.

Swallowed by the Earth

In Markland, one group of Vikings sighted five *skraelings* — a bearded man, two women and two children. They captured the two boys, but the adult natives "sank into the ground" and escaped. They took the boys back to Greenland with them where they were taught Norse and baptized. From the children, the Vikings learned that the natives had no houses but lived in caves or holes in the ground.

The Last Beothuk

When a bounty was placed on the head of every Beothuk native, it resulted in organized killings from 1613 to 1823. One Micmac trapper named Noel Boss had already killed 99 Beothuks when he came across a young Beothuk girl in the forest. He fired at her, and she was struck with buckshot. However, the girl, called Shanawdithit, escaped and grew to be a beautiful woman. Shanawdithit, the last known member of the Beothuk tribe, died in St. John's in 1829.

Before Shanawdithit died, she described the lifestyle of her people and drew pictures to illustrate her stories.

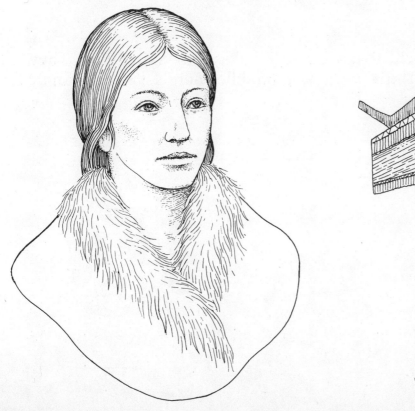

Dancing Woman

Thub-wed-gie

79

Wooden Figure

This carving, done in Thule Inuit style, depicts a person in European clothing with a cross on the chest. It was found in a tenth-century Inuit house on southern Baffin Island, called Markland in the sagas.

Iron Boat Rivets

These boat rivets held together the planks of a Viking ship. They were found on a Thule Inuit site on Ellesmere Island in Arctic Canada.

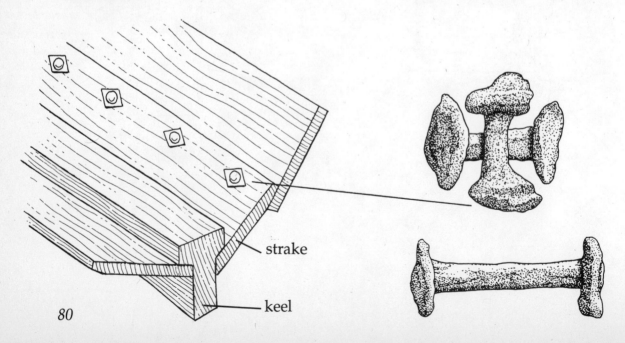

strake

keel

Rings from Chainmail

These rusted rings of iron once belonged to a Viking mail shirt or *byrnie*. They were also found at the Thule site. How do you suppose they got there?

Other Viking artifacts found in the far north include a fragment of a bronze bowl found on Devon Island and the arm of a Viking balance scale found on Ellesmere Island. On Baffin Island archaeologists found a small wood carving in the Thule style of a man in Viking clothes with a cross on his chest.

9 *The Last Voyage*

Freydis

A person who is friendly and good can inspire great happiness; a person who is unfriendly and evil can cause death and destruction. The fourth child of Eirik the Red was a daughter, Freydis, who was ambitious and ruthless.

When Karlsefni and Gudrid returned from Vinland and declared that the natives were too hostile to permit settlement, Freydis was not frightened or discouraged. She and her husband formed a partnership with two brothers named Helgi and Finnbogi, who had recently arrived from Norway. They agreed to sail to Vinland. The brothers would travel in their ship with 30 men and Freydis and her husband would take another ship, also with 30 men. In addition there was to be a small number of women in each ship. Freydis broke the agreement before they began by hiding away five extra men in her ship.

Trouble broke out as soon as they reached Vinland. Freydis insisted on living in the buildings built by her brother, Leif the Lucky. She forced the two Norwegian brothers to build their own houses farther inland.

That winter the brothers challenged Freydis and her followers to some friendly sporting contests and games to help pass the cold winter months. But the competitions turned to distrust and anger, and eventually they had to be discontinued.

The hostility between the two camps grew worse. Then one morning Freydis returned from the camp of Helgi and Finnbogi to tell her husband that they had treated her badly and struck her. It is said in the sagas that Freydis invented the story that she told her husband.

Freydis insisted that they avenge her honour. Her husband, who was feeble and weak, agreed. They attacked the other camp and killed all the men. Freydis ordered her men to kill the five women from the enemy settlement, but they refused. In a rage, Freydis killed the women herself.

When they sailed back to Greenland, Freydis demanded that her men tell no one about the killings, but the gossip spread. Eirik the Red was dead by this time and his eldest son, Leif the Lucky, was the head of the household. Leif was a person of great honour and wisdom. When he discovered the truth, he was disgusted. He declared first, that Freydis and her descendants would never prosper and second, that there would be no further expeditions to Vinland. From that time on, everyone looked down on Freydis and her family.

Therefore, it was fighting among the Vikings that caused the end of the Norse settlements in North America.

Woman Warrior

The Viking women were as hardy as the men and, in some cases, they were known to fight as well as the men.

On one occasion, when Karlsefni and his men were attacked by *skraelings*, he was forced to retreat to the edge of a cliff. All seemed hopeless, but then a Norse woman picked up the sword of a dead Viking and attacked the Indians. The natives were so alarmed at the sight of the woman warrior, they fled and the Vikings were able to escape to their ship.

Viking Sports

Archery was a favourite Viking sport, as well as a necessary hunting skill.

Weight-lifting contests, involving large boulders, were popular with the Vikings. Great physical strength was admired in both men and women.

Vinland Crossword Puzzle

ACROSS:

1. The Viking name for Labrador.
2. The name of the Viking alphabet.
3. The island that disappeared.
4. A Viking ship.
5. The king of the Norse gods.
6. The first European killed by North American natives.
7. The Viking name for a story.
8. The person who discovered North America.
9. The man who established the first settlement in Vinland.
10. Magical one-legged creature in Norse mythology.
11. The widowed daughter-in-law of Eirik the Red.
12. The home of the Norse gods.

DOWN:

3. The woman who led the last Viking expedition to Vinland.
7. The first white child born in Vinland.
13. The last Beothuk.
14. A Viking weapon.
15. The Norse god of thunder.
16. A catapult weapon used by North American natives.
17. The nickname given to Leif Eiriksson.
18. The Viking name for Baffin Island.
19. The Viking name for North American natives.
20. The last name of the man and woman who discovered the ruins at L'Anse aux Meadows.
21. The native tribe in Vinland.
22. A navigational aid used by Norse sailors.
23. The present-day name for Vinland.

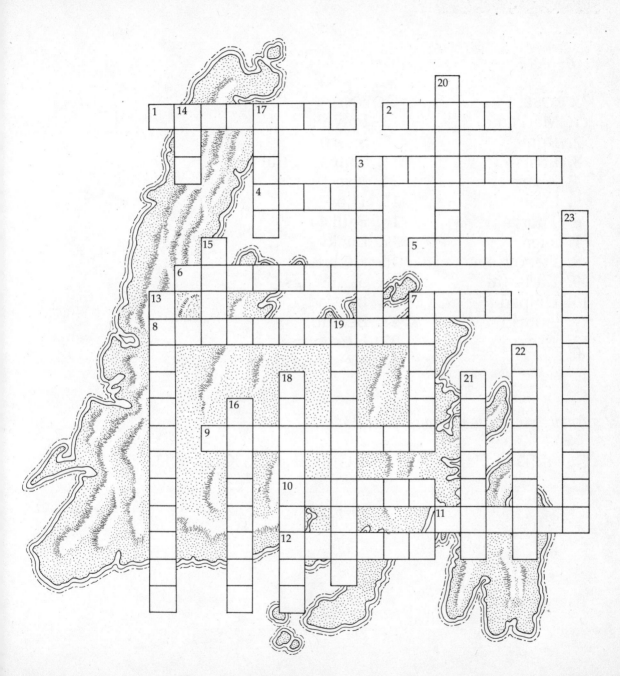

87

Answers:

ACROSS:
1. Markland
2. Runic
3. Frisland
4. Knarr
5. Odin
6. Thorvald
7. Saga
8. Herjolfsson
9. Karlsefni
10. Uniped
11. Gudrid
12. Asgard

DOWN:
3. Freydis
7. Snorri
13. Shanawdithit
14. Axe
15. Thor
16. Ballista
17. Lucky
18. Helluland
19. Skraelings
20. Ingstad
21. Beothuk
22. Husnotra
23. Newfoundland

Answer to runic message, page 23:

GUDRID IS THE PRETTIEST GIRL IN ALL ICELAND

Index